HOW TO FIND OUR V

Born in 1937, Barry Cooper lived through World War II, aware of swarms of German bombers in the sky, seeing Coventry burning in the distance. Watching endless convoys of new military vehicles passing by, from the factory at Longbridge. With his father away at war. Without really being aware of what was going on then, and only aware now of the austerity he lived through for 30 years.

His time at a private prep school, preparing for entry to a grammar school was curtailed by ear problems. Today antibiotics would deal with the problem, but this was before the NHS. His mother paid for operations, with no money left for the prep school. So Barry went to a village school and then, in 1948, on to Alcester Grammar School.

Starting work as a 16-year-old at Birmingham Corporation, he trained as a municipal engineer. Followed by National Service in the Royal Artillery, in Germany then onward and upward in local government. He was Head of Transportation at Southampton City Council, Deputy County Planning Officer at Oxfordshire County Council, and Director of Transport Studies at the University of Wales.

In desperation at the awfulness of public sector hierarchies, he and his wife set up and ran a direct marketing company. Throughout his top-down public sector career, Barry became increasingly interested in bottom-up thinking.

Research on the internet and the development of blogs oriented to bottom-up ideas led to his understanding of how top-down things work in the UK. And to this book.

HOW TO FIND OUR WAY INTO THE FUTURE

- from the grassroots

Barry Cooper

THE REAL PRESS
www.therealpress.co.uk

Published in 2023 by the Real Press.
www.therealpress.co.uk

ISBN (print) 9781912119363
ISBN (ebooks) 9781912119998

For Jae with love, and in memory of Simon who was alive when this book was being written.

Contents

Part One: How things were

Part Two: Transition

Part Three: Imagining the future

Author's note

My views on how the future will unfold are based on two blogs and a podcast. They sre:

Surplus Energy Economics by Tim Morgan.
The Consciousness of Sheep by Tim Watkins.
The Great Simplification with Nate Hagens.

Thos three have enabled me to see how the economy grew and is now shrinking.

Tim Morgan explains: "*Fundamentally, **we're at the end of a long period of rising prosperity built on low-cost energy** from coal, petroleum and natural gas. There is, as of now, no like-for-like replacement for the energy value hitherto sourced from fossil fuels.*"

Tim Watkins says: "*We have insufficient energy to power our indulgent lifestyles, and we are going to have to power down in the worst possible way, with those at the bottom starving and freezing even as those at the top attempt to cling onto their ill-gotten gains.*"

I lived through the Second World War and its aftermath. Daily life at the grassroots then helped me to imagine how the future will unfold.
Both blogs have common themes of essential and discretionary spending.

Tim Morgan's blog concentrates on the economy as an energy-based process. Anything that happens must involve using energy.

He writes that his "*main interest is in a radically new way of thinking about economics.*"

Tim Watkins "*started the Consciousness of Sheep website as an offshoot of my book of the same title. It has, however, morphed into a running commentary on the slow-motion train wreck that is Western civilisation in general and its British variant in particular*".

Nate Hagens' podcast "*explores the systems science underpinning the human predicament. Conversation topics will span human behaviour. The goal is to inform humans about the path ahead and inspire people to play a role in our collective future.*

"Simplification, beginning with the onset of financial and economic turbulence, followed by contraction.

"The ensuing simplification will be among the most

significant events ever experienced by our species.

"Those who look through a systems lens can serve as early visionaries of a simpler life with new ways of relating to technology, to consumption, to each other and to Earth's ecosystems."

I could not have written this book without the knowledge I gleaned from the two blogs and the podcast.

Foreword

The UK economy is shrinking. We are moving into a new era. An era which will be quite unlike anything we have ever known.

The old ways, which we depended on for a living, are also over.

Although no one knows exactly how the future will unfold, it is already happening. But it is difficult to see, unless you know what to look for.

This book provides pointers which will help you to understand what is happening.

The book is in three parts.

The first part is about our domestic spending behaviour since the Second World War.

Essential and discretionary spending in a smaller economy than we now enjoy

What we did as the economy recovered after the war.

How we spent our earnings.

The second part explains what I learnt from my past,

about how things connect.

- Seeing things from the grassroots.
- Essential and discretionary spending.
- The shrinking economy.
- Transition to the new ways.

The third part is my interpretation of how the future will evolve.

A shrinking economy with decreasing discretionary spending.

The disintegration of post-industrial lifestyles.

Migration to new ways of thinking, seeing and living.

A mixture of pieces about how things might be as the UK economy gets smaller. To help you think about your own and your family's future.

A mixture in no particular order. We cannot see the future as a linear sequence, as we now see the past.

In time, we will recognise how everything fits together. A new kind of logic will emerge. Of connectedness.

This is not a book about what should happen. It is about what is *already* happening and is likely to evolve.

It is not political.

It is not preaching causes, such as the need to end

growth, to secure an ecological future. Or the need to subsidise growth.

It is what we remember and learned during the years since World War II. And how this can help us to see how the future will be.

Part One
How things were

How was your past?

We can find our way into the future by reflecting on how things were in our past. It helps us understand how the economy affects our lives.

Reflecting on my own life has enabled me to write this book. I can see how economic growth dictated what happened to me and my family. This gives me insights into how the immediate future will be.

Wartime

I was born in 1937 and spent my childhood through World War II. I left school in 1953, the year sweet rationing ended. At that time, food, clothes and fuel (coal and petrol) were rationed by the government. Designed to ensure fair shares for all. Especially women and children,

At a time when resources were focused on the war, and our fathers, were away. My father, a Royal Marine officer, trained for D-Day and commanded a landing craft on Sword Beach. And was then sent to join in the war in the Pacific.

During the war, every man, woman and child was given a ration book. With coupons which enabled rationed goods to be purchased.

Basic foods were rationed during the war and afterwards until the 1950s.

Everyone had an allowance of coupons. Householders (usually wives, the husbands were away at war) had to register with particular retailers.

The weekly amounts of food per person varied from 1940 to 1954.

As an example:

Item	**Max level pw**	**Min level pw**	**April 1945**
Bacon & ham	8 oz (227 g)	4 oz (113 g)	4 oz (113 g)
Sugar	16 oz (454 g)	8 oz (227 g)	8 oz (227 g)

Item	Max level pw	Min level pw	April 1945
Loose tea	4 oz (113 g)	2 oz (57 g)	2 oz (57 g)
Meat	1s 2d	1s	1s. 2d. (equivalent to £2.68 in 2021)
Butter	8 oz (227 g)	2 oz (57 g)	2 oz (57 g)
Margarine	12 oz (340 g)	4 oz (113 g)	4 oz (113 g)
Lard	3 oz (85 g)	2 oz (57 g)	2 oz (57 g)
Sweets	16 oz (454 g) *per month*	8 oz (227 g) *per month*	12 oz (340 g) *per month*

Tinned goods, dried fruit, cereals and biscuits, were rationed using a points system.

Long queues for rationed food were common.

When the economy was as small as it was then, the

government also rationed clothes and energy supplies.

The government encouraged people to grow vegetables in their gardens and allotments.

I learned to dig and plant our vegetable garden when I was quite young.

All of this was essential spending.

Post-war hardships

When the war ended in 1945, rationing continued. Some of the food imported into Britain was diverted to Europe. This was to help feed the millions of displaced starving people who had to be fed and made safe from infection.

Food, clothes and coal were all essential to our lives. Wages were low and they were all we could afford, with a few exceptions for special occasions.

Boys were not allowed to wear long trousers until they were 12 years old. Turn-ups were not allowed on trousers and the number of pockets was restricted. This so-called Utility scheme for all kinds of clothes lasted until 1952.

This was how things were when the UK economy was only big enough to support essential spending.

Enough to provide families with a basic lifestyle.

We were used to living with just the essentials we needed for basic life.

Food rationing ended in 1954.

Coal was rationed until 1958. At that time, homes were heated by coal fires, with hot water from coal-fired boilers. Which was a problem for those who didn't have access to firewood.

I remember taking an old pram to the local gasworks to get coke (processed coal) for our kitchen stove.

With rationing over and done with, if we could afford it, we were able to spend move on food..

Family spending

Non-essential (discretionary) spending which hadn't existed in the post-war era became possible with the end of rationing.

Things became easier as the economy grew and wages grew with them.

We began to spend our surpluses on cars, holidays, home heating and eating out. It was the emergence of consumerism. Made possible by a growing economy and increasing wages.

Discretionary spending amounts varied between individuals and families. It was an inequality which grew with time.

Borrowing, consumerism, inflation and growth

From the late 1960s onwards, government restrictions on personal borrowing were relaxed and discretionary markets and spending then became possible for those who could afford it.

Buying houses with mortgages and selling them at inflated prices enabled families to release equity for use on discretionary spending.

Inflation and wage increases keeping pace made us more prosperous. Consumerism was established.

Whilst the national economy, grew prosperity increased.

Until the early 2000s.

Propped up growth

Since then we have been told by the government, the Bank of England and the media that the economy (as measured by the GDP) continued to grow.

We weren't told that this financial growth was

propped up by government quantitative easing (borrowing).

Neither were we told that, in the early 2000s, the real economy of goods and services had stopped growing. The inflated financial economy had taken over the way the figures are presented to us.

The cost of the fossil fuel energy (coal, oil and natural gas) used to generate useful energy (electricity, domestic gas, petroleum and diesel) then became more expensive than the value of the useful energy produced.

Tim Morgan points out that: "*all economic output (other than the supply of energy itself) is the product of* ***surplus*** *energy – whenever energy is accessed, some energy is always consumed in the access process, and surplus energy is what remains after the energy cost of energy (ECoE) has been deducted from the total (or 'gross') amount that is accessed.@*

There was no longer a surplus, that in the past fuelled growth.

Part Two
Transition

The old ways are done. We now need to understand how things work, to enable us to see how the future may be.

The big picture

The economy grew for about 60 years, since World War II. Then we had about 15 years of no real growth, albeit presented as growth by the powers that be, supported by the media.

Now the economy is shrinking. For the time being (in 2022), we seem to be in a recession.

The early growth in the economy was just essential spending. Followed by about 40 years of growth in essential spending and increasing growth in discretionary spending.

From now on, the process will be the reverse of the years of growth.

From the early 2020s, essential public sector

spending came under pressure from increased consumer demand. And discretionary spending and markets went into decline. This was reflected in increasing financial problems and redundancies in the so-called hospitality sector.

Discretionary spending will now decrease until it is no longer affordable. Household spending will then be limited to essentials. Which will become less affordable.

The two kinds of economy

There are at least two ways of thinking about the economy.

(1) *The money economy* (measured by the GDP) is the one we are told about. As Tim Morgan explains: "*Money has no intrinsic worth, and has value only in terms of the things for which it can be exchanged...*"
(2) *The energy economy* of goods and services. All of which require the use of energy. "*Nothing of any economic value or utility can be supplied without using energy. Energy can be defined as 'a capacity for work' and, historically, everything that we wanted or needed was produced using the labour (work) of humans and animals, plus some early application of the power of wind and water.*

That changed in the late 1700s when we learned how to deploy the vast reserves of energy contained in fossil fuel (FF) deposits of coal, oil and natural gas."

The energy economy is now shrinking. As a result, the amount of surplus energy available, after the production of useful energy is reducing.

The financial economy, as measured by the GDP, is said to be growing. But this is not real growth, because it is created by borrowing. Which can only last for as long as the government is able to borrow money.

Before long, when borrowing is no longer possible, the financial economy will shrink down to the prevailing level of the energy economy.

This will be troublesome, leading to commercial and public sector organisations failing, with consequent job losses. By the time this happens, the shrinkage could be as much as 50 per cent.

This is beyond the scope of this book. It should be borne in mind when trying to understand what is happening in the stock market.

Our mindsets

Most of us have the same mindset. It is the way

most of us think. We want our economy to grow.

- We want the safety of growth. It gives us a feeling of financial security.
- We will not normally contemplate the possibility of no growth.

Yet the UK economy is now shrinking. There can be no more growth.

To think realistically about the future, we must change our mindsets.

A symptom of the shrinking economy is declining prosperity. Increasingly we will feel worse off.

The future will be a mixture of decline followed by less growth within the overall shrinking economy, With no prospect of change. Which will be hard to get used to.

There will be continuing denial of shrinkage. Especially by those in established jobs and positions.

It is not a transition, in which we know where we are going.

Until we begin to understand what to expect it will be uncomfortable, especially for those who depend on and expect growth.

Energy blindness

Nate Hagens has drawn attention to our "energy blindness". Everything we do requires energy. Human and fossil fuel energy.

Tim Watkins in his blog has described where we are now:

" ... the fossil fuels which account for 85 per cent of the energy (nuclear and hydroelectric account for most of the rest) which powers everything we do are a precious and finite resource. And as our economic demand for growing energy supplies has been insatiable, so we have brought forward the day when it was no longer possible to keep providing additional energy... and thus economic growth."

This is the problem. There isn;t enough energy to enable us to maintain the lifestyle we are used to.

Green energy?

You may ask "what about the green energy, produced by the sun, wind and tides?"

The production of green energy is dependent on fossil fuels, to manufacture the hardware used to produce the energy. And then maintain it.

It will be impossible to produce enough alternative energy to power our existing industrial lifestyle.

Moreover, the eventual replacement of sophisticated worn-out heat pumps and the ventilation systems required to keep air-tight houses healthy places in which to live, is likely to become unaffordable.

There can never be enough green energy produced to enable our industrial lifestyle to be maintained.

Reconciliation

Sooner or later the financial economy will be reconciled with the energy economy. The financial growth mindset will then be at an end.

Tim Morgan has suggested that:

"The 'financial economy' will contract by between 35 and 40 per cent, in real terms, and on a global basis.

In Britain, discretionary consumption is projected to be 57 per cent lower in 2040 than it was in 2019.

Economic prosperity will continue to deteriorate, whilst the real cost of essentials will carry on rising."

Top-down and bottom-up mindsets

There are two fundamentally different employment cultures and associated mindsets in the UK economy.

(1) **The top-down mindset** of bosses and employees in the commercial and public sectors, and
(2) **The bottom-up mindset** of those of us who live at the grassroots. In towns and the countryside.

Unless you have experienced life in both employment cultures, you will be unable to imagine life in the "other" one.

You may be able to imagine the existence of the two ways, but don't kid yourself that you can understand how the "other" one ticks if you haven't been there.

Which doesn't matter - as long as you are aware that both exist.

This is why we have difficulty understanding each other's mindsets.

The unfolding future of top-down and grassroots spending

With the aforesaid in mind, the future in the shrinking economy can be better imagined.

The top-down aspects of our society which are dependent on growth, are now shrinking by amalgamation, delayering and redundancy.

They are:

- Top-down public sector organisations, such as local authorities and NHS bodies.
- All kinds of commercial organisations.

What they see to be the discretionary aspects of the services and businesses they provide will have a lower spending priority than essential services.

- Social ssrvice departments will stop allocating individual social workers to individual cases.
- Supermarkets will reduce the choices of food on their shelves
- The decisions made on what is essential and discretionary spending are dictated by legal constraints and commercial reasons.
- With time decisions on essential items become discretionary. For example, local authority bus subsidies - now seen to be essential - will become discretionary when another spending department, such as education, gets into financial difficulties.

Growth at the grassroots

Bottom-up doings are already developing at the grassroots.

It is an off-grid culture, of self-organising

individuals and their families.

By off-grid, I mean dwellings will have been disconnected from the top-down infrastructure. Mains electricity, water and sewage systems. Especially in low-density country areas. Where mains services were installed say 50 years ago.

Off-grid will be impossible in high-density urban areas.

The future will develop from the grassroots and it os cvery hard to imagine it. That is what the rest of the book is about.

Part Three
Imagining the future

This part of the book is a collection of pieces, long and short, illustrating how the future will develop.

Don't attempt to them as a continuing story.

The pieces are connected, but not in the hierarchical ways of the past.

There is some repetitiveness. This is deliberate, to reduce the need for backtracking, as you jump around from piece to piece.

No need to wait

I sometimes come across individuals who would welcome the idea of the future being human-based, rather than imposed on them by top-down authorities.

I don't expect employees in top-down public sector organisations to see the benefits of the future I foresee. They consider it to be a fanciful dream, that can only come in the unlikely event of the total collapse of the present system.

But there is no need to wait. It is already happening at the grassroots. If you are reading this to help find your way there, you are probably already there without realising it.

The early adopters of doings at the grassroots will get their ideas from local craftspeople, books and the internet. Connections with like-minded individuals also play a role. Top-down unemployment of thinking people will be a trigger.

I must emphasise, that by “grassroots”, I mean individuals and their extended families. Not local organisations.

It is happening now, albeit out of sight if you are not looking for it.

Choose the essential option

If you are concerned about your future, you should avoid being involved in anything to do with today’s discretionary employment and markets. Their future is uncertain.

These are the jobs which not so long ago were said to be jobs for life. They are now declining, sometimes before our eyes, such as in hospitality. They are no longer jobs for life.

Only consider working in a discretionary market if you would be happy to move on sooner or later.

If you do take one of these discretionay jobs bear in mind:

1. That daily life will become increasingly uncomfortable because the number of jobs in your place of employment is likely to decline. There will be threats of redundancy.

2. By deferring a move into self-employment, you will be less likely to be leading the way in grassroots doings in your locality.

This applies throughout the economy. Nationally about half of the economy is discretionary. If you live in the countryside, it may be much higher. Wherever you are, discretionary activities will decline, eventually to a condition much like it was in the 1950s.

At that time, farming was the main employment in country areas. Mechanisation and the amalgamation of farms put an end to that.

The shrinking economy will lead to the declining viability of industrial agriculture. Land which is unsuitable for mechanised farming will provide opportunities for small farms and smallholding startups.

Taking a job or creating a smallholding in this essential market will be worthwhile, especially for your children.

A shrinking economy

A shrinking economy is new to all of us. It is not like a conventional recession which has an end.

At present (2023), published figures for the GDP imply there is growth. But it is the financial economy which is growing, as a result of government borrowing. Which has nothing to do with your future.

Property prices will decline in a shrinking economy. Especially flats and apartments without gardens.

Country houses with gardens and land might maintain their value and will fit in well with a local food economy.

Wages and self-employed charges for work done are now (2022) often over £30 per hour.

In the 1950s, wages in local shops were around £4.00 per week. The economy was much smaller then and inflation has made it difficult to compare then with now.

In a declining economy, wages will go down. If you

are setting up a new business you should assume that this will happen.

The costs of essentials will increase if they use energy.

You should not assume that discretionary markets and jobs will exist in the future. Personal and family hobbies will be an exception. Especially for elderly and infirm people.

Bear in mind that eventually, most discretionary spending of the kind we have become used to in recent years will cease.

There will be some growth

In a local neighbourhood, where the local economy is declining, new opportunities may arise as a result of declining property prices.

Local pubs could eventually become viable again when the costs of old properties come down. Providing local beer and cider for those who regard drink and company to be essential.

Generally, small businesses should be able to take advantage of declining property prices. Providing debts is avoided.

Hierarchies and bureaucracy

In the early years of grassroots doings, individuals coming out of companies and public services will want to organise things in the ways they were used to when in top-down employment.

They may be tempted to set up their new enterprises in the hierarchical ways they were used to. With paid managers and employees.

In a shrinking economy, businesses will have to operate in a culture of declining prices.

Families and extended families will be able to operate in this culture because they have a vested interest in making their family business sustainable. Even if their wages have to reduce substantially.

Costs are liable to get out of control in a bureaucracy of employees. Growth in this kind of organisation can be an end in itself. Increasing the size of the organisation is seen to be the way to increase profits. This is incompatible with a culture of decline. Careers dependent on financial growth, will not exist in the future.

Vested interests

Vested interests motivate so much that is done. Individuals seeking power, employment, promotion and security in hierarchical organisations are motivated by their vested interests.

Everyone in a top-down organisation will have a personal vested interest in the growth and survival of their employment in the organisation.

At the grassroots, everyone will have vested interests in advancing their own and their family's interests. To avoid difficult ‘conversations’ this should be openly admitted.

There will be occasions when individuals and their families can co-operate with others to develop shared vested interests.

Individuals with hidden vested commercial interests were a problem in the past. Especially for individuals whose wealth was in the stocks and shares they held. When this happens, an individual, perhaps unknowingly, will make decisions which seem to be illogical to those who are not aware of his or her interest. In a shrinking economy, there is no financial growth, it is difficult to make financial gains. Commercial organisations dependent on getting returns on investments will have increasing difficulties.

Borrowing may be possible to finance the purchase of land for a farming business. Probably from relatives and friends, as happened in the past in the days before commercial farming.

Assets

The assets worth having in the future will be physical. Land and property will be the most useful, providing they are debt-free.

Avoid buying machinery, especially anything driven by liquid fuels or mains electricity.

It remains to be seen how the future of mains electricity will evolve, bearing in mind the high energy content required to manufacture, generate and distribute electricity. Tools using electricity will become dependent on solar-powered devices.

It may be years before daily life has reached this point throughout the economy.

Diffusion

An important step in the growth of grassroots doings will be the diffusion of the knowledge and experience of those already doing it

In the UK there is some support for localism, but it is being promoted by top-down organisations. Local information hubs may be set up by the local authority, anxious to be seen to support local communities. But their ideas about what is best for you will inevitably reflect their own best interests. They will want to make you dependent on them.

If so-called "local community development" does not come from the grassroots, it will be based on the top-down mindset of the public authority which is promoting it. This will delay the emergence of authentic grassroots growth.

In the end, subsidised development in such localities will wither away. They will lose both their top-down support (which will have to be focused on top-down essentials) and their opportunity for authentic grassroots development will be stultified.

Fossil fuel-related energy

The fact that the economy is shrinking has to be understood and accepted before the future can be seen.

It can never be possible to generate enough energy from wind, sun, water and other alternative sources to replace all the fossil fuel energy.

A society based entirely on alternatives will be much smaller than a fossil fuel-based society, of the kind we are used to.

Many things depend on oil. That cannot be replicated by an alternative.

Most bitumen is made by distilling crude oil. Road

construction is dependent on bitumen. Electric vehicles must have roads. A dichotomy which will become irrelevant.

In the long term, a society quite different from today's will emerge. Electric vehicles will be unaffordable for use in discretionary activities.

We must discount the notion of a future society which is anything like we have now.

In the imminent future dreadful weather events – heatwaves, droughts, floods, rising sea levels and storms – may result in the general acceptance of the need to eliminate the use of fossil fuels.

I doubt that this will happen before fossil fuel stops being used because it is too expensive. Alternatives which are dependent on fossil fuels for their manufacture will also cease production.

It remains to be seen how much ecological degradation will occur before the energy-based economic shrinkage will suppress the use of fossil fuels energy. A trend in this direction may already have started, prompted by increases in energy prices.

We can anticipate a future in which domestic discretionary markets and spending will not exist. We cannot look further ahead.

Food

As the economy shrinks and prosperity declines the relative importance of food products will increase.

Increasing costs of commercial food will prompt individuals and families to grow and process food, for themselves and to sell locally.

For those without gardens, access to low-cost allotments or free-to-use ground will be important. For growing and processing food for their use or selling locally.

Business redundancies will release land for non-industrial use. Which will provide opportunities for food growing and processing.

Individuals and families wanting a secure future should develop businesses growing, processing, marketing, selling and distributing food.

In rural areas, not-for-profit mutual enterprises may take over and convert large farms to organic use. Dividing their farms into smaller units. Perhaps including common land for grazing livestock.

Food and planning

My comments on a document published by Herefordshire Council's planners illustrate my thinking about how an area could become oriented to food production.

The council's local plan assumes never-ending economic growth. This is wishful thinking. Within a few years, it will be realised that economic growth is not possible. The economy is shrinking involuntarily and will continue to do so for the foreseeable future. This is not a political statement – it is how things are and will be.

The local plan must accept this as reality if the plan is to be worth doing.

The planning officers have a problem. They have to conform to the long-established culture of never-ending growth. This is how things are seen, nationally and locally.

The growth of the UK economy stopped in the early 2000s. Since then, the government, probably without realising it, has maintained a false sense of growth by borrowing money:

About £1 of growth in the GDP is created by about £4 of borrowing.

Covid-19 is said to have triggered a wave of problems. Wages have not kept up with inflation. Electricity, gas and fuel prices are increasing. Problems for which the epidemic was not to blame. They would have happened anyway, albeit a bit later. The government has continued borrowing and the myth of growth has continued.

The current state of the nation, muddling and indecision may turn out to be a symptom of the transition to a new normal.

The economy is shrinking because the energy cost of the energy which drives the economy is now insufficient to drive growth. Prosperity is declining and the cost of essentials, such as food and electricity, is increasing. Economic hardship and 'food poverty' are increasing. All symptoms of the shrinking economy.

Reductions in discretionary markets are the main aspect of the shrinking economy. Not just because the economy is shrinking, but also because the cost of essentials is increasing.

Energy costs – electricity, gas and petrol – are increasing and will do so for the foreseeable future.

Existing businesses selling non-essential (discretionary) products and services will eventually either cease trading or adapt to meet quite different demands.

Food poverty, already evident in the growing

number of local food banks, will become a major problem. It will dominate the national and local political agendas.

The Herefordshire Local Plan should confront this problem. The well-being of the population of Herefordshire is more important than continuing the charade of growth.

Faced with increasing prices of food produced commercially, the only way to reduce food prices to avoid food poverty would be to reduce or even eliminate the hidden costs involved in commercial food production. Including growing, processing, packaging, transporting, selling and managing food production and commercial costs to provide dividends for growth-hungry investors. This would be achieved by shifting growing and processing food from the conventional commercial sector to local businesses, including co-ops and self-employed and domestic gardening.

It would then be up to the initiative of residents, as individuals or in community organisations, to produce, process and distribute the food at much lower costs. This would be a huge challenge, but possible – as it was during World War 2 and the post-war period.

My vision for the plan is of a county focussed on

growing and processing food for local consumption and export to metropolitan markets. Staving off food poverty, by doing everything possible to enable residents to join in growing and processing their food.

Local economies based on food growing and processing do not exist at present, because there is no need for them. We are content to buy the food we need from the supermarkets. At present, most of us can afford to do this, but an increasing number of people will be unable to afford it.

Food poverty must be avoided by a shift in food buying to local and homegrown food. In urban areas, allotments and smallholdings will be required. Food bartering will complement conventional markets. Those who remember the 1940s and 50s will understand.

With increasing road transport costs, vegetable and fruit growers who have surpluses will look for cheaper alternatives to get their produce to metropolitan markets. Rail transport can be developed to do this.

Food producers will want to be near railway stations. As a result, the existing rail routes will become corridors of local food production businesses and associated housing development.

The existing rail networks should be electrified and light-rail (tram) routes should be built, radiating from Hereford and the market towns. To carry both goods and passengers, and powered by electricity generated by the operators.

Redundant land in the urban areas, previously used by non-essential businesses, should be converted to small-holdings and allotments. New social housing should be low density, to provide gardens, allotments and smallholdings.

This is a vision that would occur naturally to match growing demands for low-cost food and the availability of people to work on the land and in their gardens. Which will be dependent on the rate of economic shrinkage (degrowth).

Growing and processing food would lead county-wide development, with services supporting the food businesses. Not unlike the pre-industrial agrarian era, with the benefit of knowledge and know-how gained during the present era.

This post-industrial future could take years to develop or occur sooner than expected. It will be important to encourage and enable it to happen whenever the opportunity arises. Local food growing and processing must now be enabled to dominate local thinking and planning.

Avoiding widespread food poverty must be given the highest priority in the future of Herefordshire.

Policies in the Local Plan should be based on this vision of Herefordshire's future as a food-growing and processing county.

Is an ecological future possible in a global economy which is shrinking?

We must think of processes. Not end-states.

Processes which, in the UK, are the way things are already developing. Albeit not yet generally acknowledged.

If we are to imagine a future which is realistic and achievable we must also imagine how to get there. We must understand where we are now and what is going on. The future will be the natural evolution of how things are now. A non-violent revolution.

The global financial system is shrinking. Quantitative easing (printing money) is giving the impression of growth.

As a result, the top-down systems which created the growth we don't want are also shrinking.

The public sector and commercial organisations are all top-down.

The number of individuals employed in the top-down systems is declining.

The unemployed people are “moving” to the grass-roots. At first, some of them and their families are dependent on government subsidies. Later they have to learn how to join the rest, who are self-supporting. Sometimes in self-sustaining extended families. With the potential to evolve into local economies.

Not planned. They just happen

The rate of shrinkage of the UK national economy is accelerating as a result of increasing energy prices and declining energy surpluses.

Essential spending, which is dependent on energy, is becoming more expensive.

Discretionary domestic spending is declining and will soon become non-existent for the majority. As happened in the years after World War II.

Food poverty is increasing and prosperity is declining.

Social unrest is growing and will become a political problem. Worker strikes, actual and threatened, are increasing.

All of which will lead to financial, social and ecological breakdown.

In the countryside, industrial agriculture will

become unsustainable, because of the high energy costs of fertilizers and complex machinery and the cost of borrowing.

Land prices will drop and farms will become bankrupt because of rising interest rates. Land holdings will have to be broken up.

Farmers are likely to sell unproductive land to help pay their overdrafts. Creating opportunities for unemployed newcomers moving from urban areas. Individuals who are content to work for a secure livelihood rather than the insecurity of discretionary top-down employment. A feature of the shrinking economy.

Similarly, families will learn how to grow and process their food and barter their surpluses.

Local food economies will develop. Based on self-organising clusters of extended families and like-minded individuals.

All of which will naturally evolve, with no top-down planning or management.

In the long term, this may evolve into the kind of culture which Helena Norberg Hodge found in Ladakh, in the Himalayas, before it was corrupted by tourism.

In towns, like in the countryside, there will be a transition from working for failing discretionary businesses to self-employment in food businesses.

In low-density areas where houses have gardens, householders can grow their food and sell their surpluses.

In high-density areas where modern housing does not have gardens, community gardens and allotments will enable householders to grow their food. Commuting out of town to work on the land at the outside edge of town will be an option.

In the longer term, when industrial businesses in discretionary markets cease trading the land they occupy will become available for small-scale farming and allotments.

The long-term possibility for towns will be to transition to a culture similar to the countryside.

In the future sketched here, the power and influence of top-down organisations will wane as they shrink. Securing an ecological future will depend on grassroots processes.

It was the growth-oriented top-down industrial systems which were responsible for creating global warming and the prospect of eventual catastrophe. They continue to assume that growth is necessary and that borrowing money will enable growth to be maintained.

Before long, it will be accepted that the economy is

an energy system and that growth is dependent on the availability of cheap surplus energy. Which will not be available.

Top-down systems will no longer be able to drive growth.

As the Wall Street Journal has said the causes of the growth "*were industrialisation, mechanisation, electrification and automation, joined with the ability to finance such innovations [plus a colossal, rising throughput of energy, mostly from fossil fuels].*"

None of which is available at the grassroots.

It must be concluded that global economic shrinkage is leading to the gradual extinction of top-down systems and the development of bottom-up grassroots cultures.

History tells us that, before industrialisation, agrarian cultures in the UK, were naturally ecological. This is the direction in which the evolution of UK culture is heading. The population of the UK before industrialisation was about one-tenth of the population today. Therein lies a problem. How to make nsure that a shrinking economy avoids food poverty.

A humane ecological future will require people to learn to live with less. Otherwise, starvation and depopulation will occur.

Commons

Common land is privately owned land with 'Rights of Common' over the land, used most commonly in the past to graze animals. In the future, it could be used for anything to do with food growing, processing, sale and distribution.

Grazing would have to be managed in rotation. Kept apart from other farming activities.

Ownership could be a local organisation of the commoners.

First enshrined in law in the Magna Carta in 1215, Common land traditionally sustained the poorest people in rural communities who owned no land of their own, providing them with a source of wood, bracken for bedding and pasture for livestock.

Common land could fit into a shrinking economy. A local trust could have freehold ownership of the land, with rights of access by commoners to the common. Some land could be let on tenancies to individuals and families.

A problem with common land is that animal grazing and growing food do not mix. This was one reason why the commons were enclosed from the 16th century onwards.

See: https://foundationforcommonland.org.uk/a-guide-to-common-land-and-commoning

Health and well-being

The existing National Health Service, like all top-down public sector services, will shrink.

Increasing waiting times and public dissatisfaction with services are signs of services which eventually may have to be abandoned.

Introducing charges for specialist services may seem likely. But services which at first seem essential may turn out to be discretionary. People will learn to live with their incapacities.

We must not assume, in a shrinking economy, that particular services abandoned by the NHS will be taken up by private health companies.

The grassroots response to the shrinkage of conventional health services will be to develop DIY therapies to enable people to care for their own health.

The number of private self-employed and group health therapists is already increasing. An area of growth which will continue.

The care of elderly and handicapped people unable to care for themselves will eventually have to be cared for in relatives' homes.

There may be local community health and social care services, but whether these will survive financially is impossible to know. If they do, they will require co-operative management arrangements.

These will have to be flexible, allowing for the coming and going of individuals needing care.

It will be important to resist the temptation to provide buildings for these services. This would be a poor use of resources, which would be better used for caring.

The cities will become rural

Categorisation of areas into metropolitan, urban, suburban and rural is associated with the hierarchical thinking of the old ways, dating back many centuries in the UK.

It will eventually become irrelevant in the future of grassroots thinking. Areas which are currently designated urban will become transformed as a result of the transition to the new ways.

Factories, commercial businesses, offices, and supermarkets, all of which are part of industrial society will cease to be viable as the top-down systems decline and close down. These are all in today's discretionary markets.

Areas now categorised urban will become more

rural.

Manufacturing and IT businesses in existing industrial parks in country areas will change to a mixture of food growing and processing.

Tthe ground in these industrial parks may be contaminated. They could become glass house estates self-sufficient in power and water.

The GDP

The GDP is a measure used for many years to count transactions in an area or country. Using credit, it is easy to generate transactions without adding value. This is how we had the impression of economic growth.

This will be less relevant in the future. Government debts will be repaid.

Having enough to sustain your family will be important. How this will be achieved will vary. Areas close to the sea and rivers will depend on fish for their sustenance, wooded areas may depend on wild game, and other areas may develop experience in processing food grown locally.

If they exist, local currencies may be best for buying and selling local things and services.

Top-down financial services supplying credit of the kind that we are used to will not survive in a no-growth culture,

Surplus human energy

Fossil fuels powered economic activities in the past. In the future surplus, human energy will power community activities which are not financially viable. Locally generated electricity (solar and wind) may provide a limited amount of power.

Identifying your own and your family's surplus human energy will help decide what to do.

After you have completed your essential daily doings to secure your home, clothing and food.

You might use your spare time to help those unable to support themselves physically. To do things which will otherwise not be done.

Domestic spending

A way of thinking about your spending would be to decide whether something is essential or discretionary.

You may think that heating the whole of your house is essential. If you cannot afford it, whole house heating will then be seen as discretionary.

In my childhood in the 1940s, each room had one (essential) electric light, usually dangling on a cable from the ceiling. I was told to “Switch that light off” when I went from one room to another.

Now we have many more lights, currently ten in our kitchen alone.

The Overton Window

In the early years of the transition from the old ways, those who are dependent on economic growth will scoff at anyone seeking the new ways.

Don’t bother to contradict them.

It may seem difficult to understand why intelligent people fail to acknowledge that a shrinking economy is possible, let alone inevitable. It is simply not in their interest to change their mindsets.

The *Overton Window* is an idea which provides an understanding of how ideas in society change over time and influence politics. The core concept is that politicians only pursue policies that are widely accepted throughout society. These policies lie inside the *Overton Window.*

The Overton Window provides a nice explanation of why a shrinking economy is politically unacceptable at present. The public is not yet aware that it is how things are. So, the idea is unthinkable.

It is suggested that there are six degrees of acceptance of public ideas:

1. Unthinkable
2. Radical
3. Acceptable
4. Sensible
5. Popular
6. Policy

Global warming, now known as global heating by activists, began to be seen as radical when *The Kyoto Protocol* became international law in 2005. Now, in 2022, it is being half-heartedly included in UK policies.

A shrinking economy, with no more growth, is unthinkable to most people whose jobs and prosperity have a vested interest in growth. No government would dare mention it publicly, or even talk about it behind the scenes, for fear of leakage into the public domain. Just like the word 'cancer' was never uttered in polite society in the past.

Economic shrinkage will eventually be seen to be

how things are. A big jump from the old ways, bearing in mind all the hurdles involved. Including abandoning the mindset of consumerism because the rising costs of essentials make discretionary spending unaffordable.

Sooner or later, economic shrinkage will fill the window of what the general public will regard as the way things are. For this to happen it must be seen as inevitable. It is how things will be. It isn't a left or right-wing fad or a quirky idea dreamt up by a counter-cultural movement.

It will be seen at the grassroots as inevitable. It is already being seen by some.

Extended families

There is a lovely book by Helena Norberg Hodge about her life in Ladakh, the ancient enclave of Tibetan Buddhism on the Himalayan frontier. She lived there for 16 years and spoke their language fluently.

When the author first arrived in Ladakh, there was a self-sustaining culture, by western standards, of extreme poverty: "At altitudes of 10,000 feet and above, and with a growing season limited to little more than four months." Nothing was brought in.

It was a culture of extended families. Without money. Whose people, she said, “exude a sense of well-being, vitality and high spirits.” Forever singing and smiling.

And then they came to know the western lifestyle of “blind consumerism”, with tourists keen to buy examples of locally made clothes and be taken around the locality. You can imagine what happened. The Ladakhi lost their smiles: “They now find themselves ever more dependent – even for vital needs – on a system which is controlled by faraway forces.”

Maybe those who believe in the kind of future I am sketching should think about not moving away from where their roots are. The sooner a family becomes locally extended the better. Not just for the long term.

Even if you have already moved away, you and your immediate family could decide not to move again. Thereby planting the roots of an extended family. Those who believe in surplus energy economics expect troubling times quite soon. When being part of an extended family would be good.

Although we don’t know how the future will unravel, I am now certain that having relatives nearby would be much better than living amongst strangers.

The lesson I have learned is that local communities should consist of generations of extended families. They will work and play together and look after each other, naturally, And smile and sing. As the Ladakhi used to do.

This was how things were when we moved to our corner of Herefordshire. We were one of the few incoming families.

It seemed like everyone in the area was related, legitimately or not.

There were disagreements within families. Sometimes on religious grounds. We smiled on Sundays to see Baptists walking eastwards past our cottage and Primitive Methodists walking westwards, to their respective chapels.

How a shrinking economy might evolve

In the past, the UK economy was growing. Now it is shrinking. A change in mindsets is inevitable, eventually.

Locally, a shrinking economy may already be part of life. Local economies on the way out will struggle for survival. Think of the decline and disappearance of the slate industry in Wales and the cotton textile industry in Lancashire.

We should see the future transition of the UK's shrinking economy in the same way. As a mixture of areas, each with more or less shrinkage. Even some growth in well-favoured areas. In total making a nation of *de*-growth.

The establishment has yet to recognise that the economy is shrinking. Which doesn't matter, because it is happening anyway.

Fundamental changes in the past, from agrarian to industrial culture, were complex multi-faceted evolutionary processes. There was a huge variation between areas. Differences that prevailed in recent times.

Not so long ago, in the 1960s some rural areas were still farmed in ways reminiscent of 200 years earlier.

In my childhood in the 1950s living in a large industrial village, which happened to be the focus of global needle manufacture (Studley in Warwickshire) there were villages a few miles away where mains electricity had yet to arrive. The villages had mains gas generated by gas works in our village.

The shrinking economy will evolve in similarly

diverse ways. Which will be impossible to anticipate. Local economic circumstances will be one strand of the evolution.

Quotations

James Lovelock: *"Warnings that once seemed like the doom scenarios of science fiction are now coming to pass. We are entering into a heat age in which the temperature and sea levels will be rising decade by decade until the world becomes unrecognisable. We have no choice but to reduce the burning of fossil fuels or face even worse consequences."*

Andrew Nikiforuk: *"We must contract the global economy, restructure technological society and restore what's left of natural ecosystems if we want to live and breathe."*

Tim Morgan: *"The crisis caused by the coronavirus pandemic has triggered two fundamental changes that were, in reality, due to happen anyway. One of these is a systemic financial crisis, and the other is the realisation that an era of increasingly-cosmetic economic 'growth' has come to a decisive end.*

"Fundamentally, ***we're at the end of a long period of***

rising prosperity built on low-cost energy *from coal, petroleum and natural gas. There is, as of now, no like-for-like replacement for the energy value hitherto sourced from fossil fuels.*

"Whilst we might hope to find a successor to waning (and climate-harming) fossil fuel energy value, three reasonable caveats need be recognised about this hope.

"First, it is by no means assured. Second, the resulting economy is likely to be smaller, meaning poorer, than the one we have today. Third, no such transition can happen ***now***, *or spare us from the consequences of the fallacious assumption that we can rely on 'infinite economic growth on a finite planet'.*

"The fact of the matter is that ***there are no financial 'fixes' for material economic deterioration.*** *Looking for such fiscal and monetary fixes simply piles additional risk onto a global financial system already inflated beyond the point of sustainability."*

Henry David Thoreau: *"Simplify your life. Don't waste the years struggling for unimportant things. Don't burden yourself with possessions. Keep your needs and wants simple and enjoy what you have. Don't destroy your peace of mind by looking back, and worrying about the past. Live in the present.*

Simplify!"

The crashing economy

The real economy is now unravelling. Much of what was made in my lifetime is now being unmade. Not in a gentle unremarkable way, as we experienced growth. More like a series of crashes.

The first crash is already occurring, in health and social care.

In April 2021, an ex-NHS chief warned of a "*truly frightening backlog of delays in vital care*". At the same time, the New Policy Institute reported that: "*After six years of sliding backwards, child poverty is back in the 20th century, at a level last seen in the 1990s and growing at a rate last seen in the 1980s.*"

If bread was rationed, in the way that NHS services are rationed, we would learn how to bake our own. We are being forced to learn how to look after ourselves, by choosing to go privately or visit a therapist.

In frustration at being unable to find the help we want, we can be expected to find what we want on the internet and buy what we need to be able to look after ourselves.

The future of the internet is unknowable. Its survival depends on the availability of technology and satellite communications. Which in turn depends on the availability of non-fossil-fuel energy resources.

The powers that be are unwilling to admit that our NHS and Care Systems have reached the ends of their existence. They will never admit this whilst they see a glimmer of hope for their future employment.

Individuals are leaving the health and care services and the recruitment of replacement staff is not keeping up. We are told about government successes in meeting their targets for recruitment, mostly from overseas, but we are not told about redundancies, retirements and resignations.

Care staff and supermarket shelf stackers receive roughly the same pay. Both work in hierarchical organisations.

Shelf stackers quickly know intuitively what has to be done.

Support staff in care homes have to work within written protocols laid down by the national care inspectorate. They are expected to find their way through the protocols. Common sense is not expected.

Care staff have to write notes on how they spend every minute of their days. Just in case there is a problem.

Social care

There will be an increasing number of old people with physical difficulties and individuals of all ages with learning difficulties. All are unable, to greater or lesser ability, to care for themselves..

Mindful people might agree that the increasing dependence on the state, which most of us have 'enjoyed' for all our lives, is now going into reverse.

In the future of no growth, the problem of how to manage the increasing demands for social care is intractable with the current system.

It will be up to us, as individuals, families and local communities to look after ourselves. In our health, work, social and cultural activities and especially in old age.

The problem then is how to manage this move towards local community care. It has to happen. The longer the delay, the greater the problem will be.

It can't be left to a local market. It doesn't exist in care.

Local community-based organisations will have to take the lead in providing and managing care services.

Relatives of those needing care will have to become part-time or full-time carers.

Full-time caring for elderly parents in your own home is understandably unpopular in the modern UK culture, in which more than one income is essential for comfortable living.

Not only is it unpopular, but it is also impracticable with an ageing population in which very old people have to be looked after by old people.

There is an alternative but it isn't legally possible at present. Local government funding processes, Care Quality Commission inspection and regulatory systems, the personal taxation system and employment laws, all inhibit breaking away from how things are done now.

An alternative would be to use the grey economy locally.

The informal or grey economy is neither taxed nor monitored by any form of government. It is out of general sight.

If the grey economy was made legitimate it would enable volunteers, relatives and friends, to be 'employed' in care homes which are struggling financially. And providing support in residents' own homes, on very low wages. Undertaking cooking, cleaning and maintenance.

Carers in the grey economy would be paid low wages (say £2 per hour) and receive out-of-pocket expenses, on such things as travel, special clothing and meals at the home.

This approach to care cannot be legitimate in the conventional economy. I guess it is going on undercover.

Supporting people to stay in their own homes will be essential.

People become unwilling to remain in their own homes as they get old. Not just those needing care and help to look after themselves. Often it is because help is needed to look after their homes.

People become unable to deal with the day-to-day problems of living in and maintaining their houses and gardens. Changing a light bulb is a problem for those unable to balance on a chair or steps. Reaching things on top and bottom shelves becomes impossible as you get older.

People who have tended their gardens all their lives can't bear to see their cherished borders become weed infested. Aspects of daily life which are seen by younger folk to be trivial become all-consuming problems in old age, leading to a wish to move out if help is not available.

Those who become unable to grow their veg and salads are particularly sad to lose that ability. Which is so helpful in old age.

Electricians, plumbers and builders may already provide their services free of time charges to their relatives. Those without relatives locally do not get this benefit and end up in despair at their inability to care for their property.

Local community care must deal with this problem.

Trust is all important. Knowing that someone at the front door comes from the local community organisation. And that organisation is known to be trustworthy.

For local community care to be legitimate. Within the law, there is a problem. There are few formally constituted local organisations in most areas, which are empowered to undertake the kinds of services described here.

How will they get started?

To be legitimate, local organisations will need lawyers or capable individuals to set them up. They will have to make their doings financially viable. Not by conventional grants and loans, but by raising money and developing resources locally.

Not by borrowing money – this leads down conventional pathways with the potential for disaster.

They must be able to survive free of payments to members.

In the early days of local community development, local authorities might help to establish and incorporate local organisations.

Little new legislation would be needed. Just changes in mindsets.

Make sure that it becomes part of the day-to-day community. Not seen as charitable work for "the poor". Wealthy people need just as much care in old age as people not so well off.

When it is found to work, it will point the way to a new kind of future for all kinds of public services as their funding dries up.

It would be a future in which power would be transferred from public authorities to individuals and their local communities. It would contribute to a fundamental system change. It will challenge established notions that "professionals" know what is best for us.

Heating your house

During the next decade of de-growth and declining prosperity, some of the things we regard now as essential will become discretionary. How we used to live, day-to-day, at home is an example.

Until the early 1960s, houses were not centrally heated. Then, houses were built with "background" heating, with a radiator in the two rooms used for dining and sitting. And an open fire in the sitting room lit only when the room was occupied. With no heating upstairs.

As energy costs increase, we will have to find ways

to live comfortably in cold weather.

Before central heating, in many old houses, we kept ourselves comfortable by wearing warm clothes. Often including hats, even indoors.

We were physically active. Growing some of our food. Chopping wood. Shovelling coal into coal scuttles which were carried to the fireplace. All essential in those days. Actively keeping warm and healthy.

Our houses were drafty, with windows that rattled in the wind. Doors to the outside were particularly drafty because they had to open over uneven floors. Sausages made of hessian, enclosing sawdust, straw or wool, to reduce the drafts, were common.

Air movements between rooms were noticeable, with frequent admonishments to “shut that door”.

In future, faced with declining prosperity and increasing energy costs, heating our houses - seen to be essential now - will become unaffordable and will come to be seen to be discretionary.

Radiant heating, using electric radiators and open fires is a very acceptable alternative to whole-house heating.

If you are young and have land, plant hardwood (especially oak) saplings. Thin them out as they grow. Firewood will become more worthwhile as fossil fuel costs increase.

Daily life is already a complicated mixture of essential and discretionary spending. There may be a general return to how things were in the past as prosperity declines, the cost of essentials increases and discretionary spending and related markets decline.

Building homes

Those of us without a vested interest in growth will now see increasing symptoms of no growth, especially in prosperity.

Strikes, protest gatherings, and disturbances (in 2022) in France, Greece, Italy, Spain and the UK are all about people having less money to spend. In the UK, the decline of high street retailing is because people have less to spend. None of which is to do with Brexit, even though it may be blamed. All are symptoms of no-growth in prosperity.

In this piece, I raise awareness of the possible impact of no growth on UK housing. I focus on housing because it, with food, is essential to our well-being. Also, it is easier for me to imagine real physical manifestations, rather than abstract measures such as GDP which are meaningless in this context.

I have experienced no-growth.

We must understand the relationship between growth and borrowing.

Tim Morgan has written: "*Leaving theological and ethical issues aside, we need to be clear that the process of borrowing and lending is a product of growth because debt can only ever be repaid (and, indeed, serviced) where the prosperity of the borrower grows over time.*"

I lived through around a quarter century of no growth in prosperity, albeit much of it as a child during World War II. Then, throughout the austerity of the post-war era, the only houses I remember being built were council houses, including much-loved prefabs.

In the 1960s, we bought, for cash, a holiday cottage in Mid-Wales, when empty cottages could be bought for a pittance. We bought one made entirely of slate, with mains services, for £120. At that time and in that area, a new build was not financially viable, because the market value of new houses would have been less than the construction cost. That is how things are in an area of no growth.

In the same era, we bought a new house, with a mortgage, on an estate in Hampshire, for £5,000. A new build not much bigger than the cottage in Wales. Prosperity was expected to grow in Hampshire and 100 per cent mortgages were available (at 2.5 times income). Developers were able to make a profit, so they built houses.

In our culture, economic growth, borrowing and housing development are inextricably connected.

The point is that in areas of no growth, private housing development of the kind we have become used to does not occur. Property prices are insufficient for development to be commercially viable. This is nothing to do with planning policy, it is how the housing market works.

This is not to suggest that, when no growth becomes generally accepted as the UK norm, there will be no commercial housing development. There will still be areas where growth is expected and development will be seen to be financially worthwhile. Elsewhere, it will be up to the public sector to provide houses, as happened in the past when there was no growth.

But when there is no growth, will the public sector

be able to borrow to build houses?

All sorts of questions are begged!

Clusters

The world is full of clusters. They have been around since the beginning of time. They can be seen from both the top-down and bottom-up. From the bottom up you may belong to a cluster, from the top down clusters may be seen as an implicit part of economic and cultural development. Whether you expect a future of no growth or not, clusters will be part of the future.

Clusters of people and organisations are to be found in academic organisations, computer software, housing development, cybernetics, economic development, city planning, and so on.

Clusters which develop naturally bring together like-minded individuals and organisations, with common aims and values, which come together for mutual benefit. It is a togetherness which is seen by those involved as an explicit cooperative process of personal and business development. A kind of development that those involved expect to be sustainable. A kind of sustainability which complements ecological sustainability.

In my lifetime, I have known some local clusters. I will pick out three.

My childhood was spent in Studley, Warwickshire. Said at one time to be the largest village in England. Where all kinds of needles used to be made.

The first needle makers moved to Studley in the 17th century. They were families who learnt to make a living by joining an emerging cluster of cottage industry businesses with a common business interest. Known collectively as "needle ticklers", they included drillers, eyers, headers, pointers, straighteners, polishers and other specialisms. The number of needle families proliferated and then mechanisation, using water-powered mills at first, led to mergers and takeovers.

Eventually, there were just a few large businesses in factories, one of which, in the 1960s, was said to be the largest needle factory in the world.

Bigness led to a lack of competitiveness and demise. In 2007 the last needles were made in Studley. The co-operative business culture of the cluster had evaporated.

In Hay-on-Wye (population 1,500), there are over 20 books shops. A cluster started by the self-proclaimed King Richard Cœur de Livre (Richard Booth) in 1977 to counter the declining fortune of the market town of Hay (population:1,500). This cluster of booksellers 'saved' Hay, which now gets over 500,000 visitors a year. Now perhaps in decline with antique shops taking over.

Clusters emerge as happenstances. In my area, a redundant local authority village school was purchased and developed as a Steiner Academy. This led to a cluster of families with a shared interest in Steiner education.

In recent years, the emergence and development of clusters have not been recognised by the top-down land use planning system. This is particularly noticeable, sadly, with family clusters. Development control policies have, in effect, stopped families from building homes nearby for their children and aged parents. Thus exacerbating the housing and social care crises.

Clusters will become increasingly important in a no-growth world, in which people and businesses with shared values may see cooperating with like-minded people to be more worthwhile than going it alone..

The development of clusters, in response to declining wealth with new kinds of markets emerging, implies a fundamental re-think of how our lives will be organised. Maybe this is already happening, but not yet seen as such.

Declining disposable incomes will force family lifestyles to become more co-operative. Families will prefer to stay together, to support each other, rather than disperse and lose contact, as has happened during the last 50 years or so. Sustainability through togetherness will be more important than chasing a career.

Business plans can be expected to include building houses to rent to their employees. As happened in my childhood when home ownership was beyond the means of the majority.

With no growth, domestic car ownership will decline and human energy (walking and cycling) will be the way to enable travel within the clusters, to visit relatives and go about your business.

The *Institute for the Future* website shows how clusters have become a fundamental aspect of thinking about the future.

Tim Morgan has provided a convincing scenario of how the future will be in a no-growth economy. He makes the point that *"true sustainability is going to require profound structural changes, including radical reform of patterns of habitation, work and leisure*". This sounds like clusters to me.

I don't believe that any government would have electoral support for fundamental structural changes. But that shouldn't be necessary if the way forward were to be seen to be based on self-generating clusters. A process of organic development is already happening, albeit frustrated by top-down intervention.

Clusters would also make local housing more affordable and help to deal with the social problems of an ageing population.

Urban dispersal would be part of the evolution of population patterns based on clusters.

Clusters include individuals and organisations of widely differing academic and political views. They all agree that their cluster is necessary, and they all participate in the doings within it.

Clusters may be funded by other clusters, they may be agglomerations of like-minded co-operating businesses, charities or community organisations. Aligned in endless ways. They are not above each other. They are directly or indirectly connected horizontally.

They crop up in so many ways. Mental care clusters

are groups of people with similar characteristics, as identified from a holistic assessment, using a Mental Health Clustering Tool (MHCT).

The Quantum Foundations Research Cluster at Wolfson College, University of Oxford, "*unites members from the Computer Science, Materials, Mathematics, Philosophy, and Physics Departments of the University, making it an interdisciplinary activity unique in its kind.*"

Denial

The UK and further afield are in denial – about much which affects our lives, now and in the future.

Politicians, bureaucrats, industrialists, financiers, NGO employees, teachers and everyone in jobs and paid retirement they see to be safe, have a vested interest in things remaining unchanged.

This overwhelming denial can be seen as a symptom of fundamental change. Our culture is changing. It is an ongoing process. Not a transition, which implies we know where we are going. It is a change to we know not what – a fundamental change, which is denied. A change which is uncomfortable for many of us to accept.

The list of individual denials is wide-ranging. Together they add up, to an extraordinary and difficult-to-grasp change. In the cultural, economic, environmental and physical nature of our future being. Here is a short list:

DENIAL: The economy is energy-based

Tim Morgan's blog (*see appendix*) is the best introduction to this. The crucial outcome of this fact is that our present lifestyle is unsustainable.

Eric Horne points out that "*economists around the world have got it all wrong by f*ocusing on money as the key driver of economies ... *money is the language rather than the substance of the real economy. The real economy is a surplus energy equation, not a monetary one, and economic growth, as well as the increase in population since 1750, has resulted from the harnessing of ever-greater quantities of energy.*"

DENIAL: Artificial Intelligence (AI) must be controlled otherwise it could be catastrophic for the human race.

Professor Stuarts Russell's book *Human Compatible: Artificial Intelligence and the Problem of Control* which *The Guardian* says is "The most important book on AI this year" poses the prospect that AI research in its current form could be catastrophic for the human race.

A piece in *Computer World* asks: "Will AI drive the human race off a cliff?"

Naturally, this is denied by those involved in AI research, with an obvious vested interest in their work, rather than where it is leading.

DENIAL: Electric vehicles (EVs) are not the answer

As Tim Morgan has pointed out: *"EVs are a form of denial over the pressing need, which is to readdress and redesign patterns of travel and habitation that are being rendered unsustainable by energy pressures."*

Cars, of any kind, have created a way of life which is socially divisive (when did you last stop to talk to someone in another car?). Cars use energy wastefully (to build roads, manufacture cars and make electricity to power them). They encourage a sedentary lifestyle, which damages our health and, with traffic accidents, impose costs on the NHS.

Hans-Werner Sinn, Professor of Economics at the University of Munich, makes the point that: *"EVs also emit substantial amounts of CO_2, the only difference being that the exhaust is released at a remove – that is, at the power plant. As long as coal- or gas-fired power plants are needed to ensure energy supply during the "dark doldrums" when the wind is not blowing and the sun is not shining, EVs, like ICE vehicles, run partly on hydrocarbons. And even when they are charged with solar- or wind-generated energy, enormous amounts of fossil fuels are used to produce EV batteries in China and elsewhere, offsetting the supposed emissions reduction."*

The scale of the transition from combustion to electricity-powered transport is huge. Average household electricity demand could double once EV charging is included, and this will place extra strain on both the grid and energy bills.

DENIAL: Climate change cannot be stopped

It seems to be generally assumed, incorrectly, that a carbon-neutral future is possible, as a result of which global warming will be stopped. The reality, as pointed out by Prof James Lovelock in his book *Novacene: The Coming Age of Hyperintelligence,* is that we must now plan for the unavoidable outcomes of climate change.

It is physically impossible to replace all primary fossil fuel energy with renewables and maintain our present lifestyle. What this means is that we have to look at downsizing, shrinking, and using less.

DENIAl: Economic growth is no longer possible

Open Democracy, an independent global media platform has pointed out that "De-growth is the only way forward." We must plan for and get used to doing less. We don't need growth to reach a good life for all. What we do need is a genuinely democratic and radical transformation of our economy.

DENIAL: Prosperity is declining

More energy is required to produce useful energy than the energy that is produced.

The net effect is that prosperity is declining and will

continue to do so. The public knows that this is happening. As evidenced by the unrest in European countries. The establishment behaves as though it is not happening.

The government fails to adopt policies appropriate to falling prosperity and persists with policies which are either counterproductive or irrelevant.

DENIAL: Farmers' land banks stop local food production

Inheritance tax rules encourage farmers to create "land banks", which reduces access to small areas of land for start-up small-holdings and farms. Innovations which could produce food locally, that large farms would not find to be financially viable.

Car-free or not

Whether you have and drive a car is for you to choose.

If we are to cope with climate change we must rid ourselves of all spending which has a carbon-polluting effect.

All cars, not just those driven by carbon fuels, spoil our daily lives. They have created and perpetuated a divided society – anti-co-operative, accident-threatening and unhealthy.

If you see cars as essential to your lifestyle, like most car owners, you will argue that cars do much more than provide transport. They give you a sense of freedom. You can go almost anywhere, at any time.

You may deny the need to do anything to cope with climate change. You are happy to let the powers that be do something about it.

In any event, car ownership and use will become unaffordable for an increasing number of individuals and families.

In a few years, you may not be able to afford to own a car. Especially an electric car.

If you have a car now, you should decide whether to change your lifestyle. You must choose a lifestyle which suits you and your family.

I think the future will, in some ways, be similar to the days before cars dominated our lives. But not in most ways.

Imagine a future in which you will not be able to

afford a car. When you will only be able to afford essentials. There is much for you and your family to discuss.

A brief for future planning

For most people, the future will be car-free.

Some years ago, I imagined *a brief* for inventors, planners, architects and politicians. It could also be a starting point for group discussion.

Imagine a process to accommodate unavoidable future change:

- **Global heating and climate change:** These are inevitable and must be planned for.
- **Prosperity:** Will decline for the foreseeable future.
- **Capitalism:** As we know it now, will gradually collapse. This is not a political proposal – it will happen naturally. Co-operative mutualism will emerge.
- **Public spending:** Will be reduced and will have to be concentrated on health care.
- **Food production:** Will gradually be de-industrialised. Domestic food production will become essential as prosperity declines.

- **Telecommunications:** Will decentralise. Locally inspired systems will develop. Such as long-range wi-fi and communications systems such as the 'message handling service' (MHS) of the 1980s.

As always, throughout history, communications systems will determine how the post-industrial culture will develop.

Localism means we must simplify our language.

As I have got older, things have become more complicated. We now live in a world where complexity prevails. Maybe it is time to unwind?

When I was a local government officer, I didn't realise that when I was speaking to 'the public', I was not generally understood. Now I am amongst the public I cannot understand what the officers are writing and saying to me. Even when they are experts in the profession I used to know so well.

Things have moved on. Local government planning and management processes have become so complex (partly because of IT algorithms) that the professions cannot understand each other. It is also in their interests, to protect their territories.

It is not just the language that is used, it is also the procedures and the jargon. Some of which have come about as a result of ever more legislation.

A few years ago, I had to learn about the Court of Protection welfare deputyships and how to apply for one. I did it myself because I was unwilling to pay a solicitor to do it. Now I find myself in the 'privileged' position of understanding a bit of legalese that most ordinary people are not even aware of.

Not that it did me much good. Those who ought to understand when I use it listen patiently, and then ignore what I have said. Just as I used to behave as a local government officer.

Furniture makers have always had their jargon and are respected for the quality of workmanship they produce. Their complex understanding and learnt experience of their craft produces often lovely pieces of furniture. Which we can appreciate and respect without understanding how to do it ourselves.

But you cannot respect a social service 'enabler' who doesn't produce anything we find useful.

Our parish council was persuaded by someone to produce a Neighbourhood Plan. A document intended to say where the 25 or so houses to be built in the parish in the next 20 years should be put.

The planning process required by the county council was totally beyond the capability of the chairman and clerk of the council. So the clerk resigned and, without consultation with parishioners, the county Association of Parish Councils took the job over and gave it to professional planning consultants.

The county association shouldn't have done this, but what else could have been done when the county council had produced a how-to set of instructions which are beyond the ken of local folk? Including me, a one-time planner.

Of a similar ilk, I remember, in the 1970s, attending a local meeting about where to put some houses. Someone in the audience protested that this should have been the responsibility of the local populace, not the arrogant planners. In the same era, I remember a traffic commissioner criticising a bus company for taking a 'parochial view', which was not in the interest of the wider community.

Is 'parochial' good or bad? It depends on where you sit. Different perceptions and different uses of language.

The languages used by public servants are beyond common understanding. Not only do lay people not understand what is being said, but also ‘experts’ from different disciplines don’t understand each other. Which must be wasteful. No wonder so much time is spent in meetings.

Time is wasted trying to understand what is being said. We suffer from the lack of a language we all understand. Even different understandings of what words mean.

Down here, at the grassroots, we ought to be able to understand what is going on. But we can’t, when the decisions which we want to understand are made both above us and outside our language.

It is worse; we don’t know what we don’t know.

We don’t want the language used ‘up there’ to be brought ‘down here’, as happened with neighbourhood planning.

We must find our ways of doing things, guided by thinking people who live roundabout. Which requires simplification.

We must avoid the complicated and pretentious ways of talking, so beloved by professional and academic people. A spade must be understood by everyone to be a digging tool. This is not a disparaging remark!

We have visited complexity. I have had enough of it. It is now time to revisit simplicity.

Passive houses

Twenty-five years ago. my wife and I invested in an air-to-air heat pump in our new house. With heat recovery and ventilation provided by ducts. Insulation in the walls and roof, air-tightness and double-glazing.

Not up to passive house standards, having the same characteristics.

What to do when the technology needs replacement?

Building and improving UK houses to passive house standards are seen by the government, opposition parties and "the green lobby" to be an essential element of the move to net zero greenhouse gas emissions.

It is said that "a passive house uses only one-tenth of the energy consumed by an average house. With very little maintenance and upkeep. Passive houses are future-ready and will work continuously for years to come."

After 20 years of use, our system needs to be replaced. For £15,000. Which is expensive. We are in our eighties. It is not worth doing.

So we are replacing just the heat-recovery system, for £5,000, which will provide ventilation and we will heat the rooms we use with infrared radiators.

I can't imagine what we would have done if we couldn't afford £5,000.

We have to put in the heat-recovery system because ventilation is essential in an air-tight house if unhealthy mould is to be avoided.

I remember visiting the Centre for Alternative Technology in Wales in its early days and seeing a demonstration building which was insulated but had no ventilation, and the walls inside were covered in black mould.

According to the World Health Organisation, "a large chunk of the world's 300 million cases of childhood asthma is linked to prolonged exposure to indoor dampness and mould."

According to *Homebuilding and Renovating Magazine:* "Less than 200,000 heat pumps are thought to have been installed in UK homes since 2000, and around 27,000 are currently being installed each year."

According to Evergreen Energy: "Heat pumps currently last around 20-25 years before they need replacing."

According to Home Inspection Insider.Com "Insulation can last for 80 to 100 years under the right conditions. However, insulation can start to degrade in as little as 15 years if moisture or rodents are present. If your insulation is damaged to the point that it no longer provides the insulating value once intended, you should replace the insulation."

Houses are now being built or modernised that will in 25 years be subject to prolonged exposure to indoor dampness and mould with a risk of childhood asthma if their heating and ventilation systems are not replaced.

Will the owners of these houses be able to afford to replace their heating systems?

Will it be physically possible to replace the insulation of houses which have not been properly installed or maintained?

What will the state of the economy be 25 years hence?

Should we assume ongoing economic growth? Or will the calculations of degrowth made by those of us who see the economy as an energy system turn out to be correct?

Which set me thinking.

According to Renewables First, the Hydro and Wind Company: "The design life of a good quality modern wind turbine is 20 years. Depending on how windy and turbulent the site is, the turbine could last for 25 years or even longer, though as with anything mechanical, the maintenance costs will increase as it gets older."

So, it is not just the houses that will be on their last legs.

This reminds me that in the 1960s, as a Highway Engineer, I was designing roads sufficient to carry traffic only 20 years ahead. No wonder we now have congestion and pollution.

Will the same fate be suffered by today's passive houses in 25 years? Will they still be fit for healthy human habitation?

Houses built hundreds of years ago are still fit to live in. They have been kept in a fit state by successive owners according to the condition they wanted and what they could afford. They didn't plan, they did what they wanted at the time they did it.

The introduction and development of economic evaluation processes killed the old ways of deciding things.

In the old ways, they built what was wanted "now". At that time.

Economic ideas of putting value on the future with a fixed design life were then introduced.

To justify capital spending future benefits are calculated. Roads are planned to carry estimated traffic volumes 20 years later.

Then what? It is assumed that money will be available to make good the problem.

We don't know in what state the economy will be in 25 years. Will the occupants of the house be able to afford to deal with the problem?

We must plan for NOW, just like they did in the past.

Instead of planning to stop global warming, we should adapt our homes to deal with the problems we have NOW. Heat waves, flooding, unaffordable heating bills, droughts and insufficient space to accommodate homeless relatives and declining prosperity.

With that attitude, passive houses, sustainably planned for years to come, shouldn't get a look in. We should build what we want NOW.

If you believe that the economy is shrinking, discretionary spending is becoming unaffordable and essentials are becoming more expensive. We will probably revert naturally to the well-proven lifestyle of our predecessors. Wearing warm clothes, living in sometimes chilly, naturally ventilated houses. In which I was happy to live 60 years ago.

It is time NOW to abandon the idea that all new houses must be airtight with ventilation. It is up to individual occupants to decide what is wanted.

If I am right and the economy is driven by declining surplus energy, most of us will be looking for new ways to keep warm quite soon.

We should have metal or masonry chimneys. Open fires and stoves to provide radiant heat for warmly-clad people. Using smokeless fuel. And seal the drafty gaps which annoy us.

Doing what we NOW need for a comfortable and affordable life.

Heading towards the end of our industrial economy

"To put it in terms that even an economist might grasp, all energetic systems – including industrial economies – eventually burn themselves out. Ours is no different."

That is how one of Tim Watkin's posts finishes. Which set me thinking afresh about the future.

Maybe we should think about the end of our industrial economy. Rather than saving the planet.

As the economy shrinks conventional unemployment will increase.

Discretionary businesses and employment will decline. To how it was in the immediate post-WW2 era.

Employment in essential markets will decline, as a result of increasing energy costs.

Total energy use will decline. As a result of the decline, and associated emissions, the prospect of global disaster will become less threatening.

There will then be mass unemployment, declining

prosperity and increasing food poverty.

The issue will then be what to do about unemployment.

Eventually, the government will become aware that the shrinking economy is unstoppable.

The time will then have come to switch the emphasis from saving the planet to saving the people.

It will be time for a paradigm change.

To what Nate Hagens has called "The Great Simplification".

Attempts to reverse the growth-oriented industrial economy will be seen to be wasteful spending. It is already shrinking.

Large-scale industrial agriculture will be in decline. Related debt repayments will force landowners to sell their land.

Imagine if:

- To deal with increasing food poverty, the government introduces policies which support small-scale farming and smallholding. Using minimal fossil fuel-based processes.

- Redundant employees in shrinking discretionary markets switch to food growing, processing and marketing,

- Redundant urban land is taken over by food businesses.

- Local food economies develop, with associated support services.

A paradigm switch from the present industrial system to an agrarian system. Taking years to evolve. Or maybe not so long?

I can imagine how employment will switch to the new paradigm. But the rest of the paradigm is unimaginable.

With hindsight, I could not have imagined the future, back in the 1950s, when I had neither central heating, a car, a TV nor a telephone. It just happened.

The future will just happen. There's no point in thinking about it being at all like how things are now.

Turning the clock back: To a positive future at the grassroots

Most of us believe that the present recession will end. They always have in the past.

Whether it is a traditional recession and recovery or the unravelling of the system as envisaged by Tim Morgan is irrelevant for the time being. Both start the same way. As a shrinking process.

It will be a longer-than-usual process. We must now turn our mental clock back. And think about the reverse of how the economy grew in the past.

For maybe 25 years after World War II growth in the domestic economy was limited to essentials. Discretionary (non-essential) spending was almost non-existent. Except for those who were well off.

Then, consumerism burst upon us in the late 1960s. Discretionary spending gradually grew until it was about half of the UK's total spending. We bought cars, wined and dined and had holidays in faraway places.

Growth occurred in cycles of recession and recovery – decline and growth – within a process of overall growth.

In the 2000s, growth became dependent on government borrowing (quantitative easing).

Gradually, a gap of about 40 per cent developed between the financial economy propped up by QE and the real economy of goods and services. As a result, a misleading impression of economic growth was created.

The financial economy, boosted by lending, was growing. The real economy of goods and services was shrinking.

The economy is now in distress. Inflation is outpacing wages. It is beginning to be realised that wage settlements can only be paid for by further QE. Otherwise, employment shrinkage cannot be avoided.

All symptoms of the shrinking economy.

According to CBI director-general Tony Danker: "*Britain is in stagflation – with rocketing inflation, negative growth, falling productivity and business investment.*"

So, what now?

Quantitative Tightening (QT) will probably be

applied. According to Wikipedia: "*whereas QE (quantitative easing) caused the substantial rise in asset prices over the past decade, QT may cause broadly offsetting effects in the opposite direction.*"

The value of ***assets*** will now gradually decrease. By up to about the 40 per cent, referred to earlier.

We don't know how long this reconciliation between the two economies will take. It will be hidden within the overall shrinkage of the economy.

To understand how the process of shrinkage may develop we must think back to what happened during the growth of the economy.

We are now approaching the end of a period dominated by essential spending, with discretionary spending, and associated employment now in decline. The opposite of 50 years ago.

The costs of essentials are increasing and families are reviewing their discretionary spending. Which is becoming increasingly unaffordable.

Further economic shrinkage and declining wages will worsen the current mêlée.

The reality of what is going on is confused by inflation.

At the grassroots

Migration from top-down jobs, especially from discretionary markets, will generate new grassroots activities.

All kinds of activities. Employment, self-employment, undeclared work, unpaid caring and bartered activities.

New individual and collaborating businesses will develop.

Local economies will develop and grow. Mostly in essential markets. Food growing, processing, selling and distributing and related support services.

Wages for those coming down from top-down jobs will be much lower than they had before.

The consumer culture of the industrial era will not exist.

Think back to 60 years ago, when average wages were about £1,000 per annum and new houses cost less than £4,000. That is where we are headed.
My experience of life in the UK when the economy was much smaller than today, was that it was much nicer!

And finally...

The essential issue underlying my views is that if we, individuals and families, are to make life as comfortable as possible, we have to start thinking and planning for it now.

We should now decide that climate change is inevitable and plan for what we, individuals and families, should do to deal with it.

There are many ways of planning for this future, but the future itself is unstoppable.

The most important aspect of planning your future is to be aware of the difference between essential markets and how to use them and discretionary doings.

Don't waste your time and money doing things which are not essential.

Bear in mind that the economy is an energy system because nothing that has any economic value can be produced without it. There will be less of it available in the future. Use less and you will be better off.

Appendix
References

Surplus Energy Economics:
https://surplusenergyeconomics.wordpress.com/

The Consciousness of Sheep:
https://consciousnessofsheep.co.uk/

The Great Simplification:
https://www.thegreatsimplification.com/

The Real Press

www.theRealPress.co.uk

Printed in Great Britain
by Amazon

38627767R00067